Solutions for Modern Learning

Claim Your Domain—And Own Your Online Presence

Audrey Watters

Solution Tree | Press

Copyright © 2016 by Solution Tree Press

All rights reserved, including the right of reproduction of this book in whole or in part in any form.

555 North Morton Street
Bloomington, IN 47404
800.733.6786 (toll free) / 812.336.7700
FAX: 812.336.7790
email: info@solution-tree.com
solution-tree.com

Printed in the United States of America

19 18 17 16 15   1 2 3 4 5

Library of Congress Control Number: 2015948500

ISBN: 978-1-942496-23-6 (perfect bound)

Solution Tree
Jeffrey C. Jones, CEO
Edmund M. Ackerman, President

Solution Tree Press
President: Douglas M. Rife
Senior Acquisitions Editor: Amy Rubenstein
Editorial Director: Lesley Bolton
Managing Production Editor: Caroline Weiss
Senior Production Editor: Christine Hood
Proofreader: Tara Perkins
Cover Designers: Rian Anderson & Abigail Bowen
Text Designer: Rian Anderson

Acknowledgments

A special thanks to Kin Lane, who first convinced me to buy my own domain.

Table of Contents

About the Author vii

Preface ix

Introduction: The Manila Envelope 1
    Where Is the Digital Manila Envelope? 2
    Creating the Digital Manila Envelope 5
    Claiming Education Technology 6
    Chapter Overview 7

Chapter 1: The Learner's Digital Domain 9
    What Data "Count" as Education Records? 11
    Why Education Data Matter 13
    Who Owns Student Data? 14
    Claiming Student Data 17

Chapter 2: Why Claim Your Domain? 19
    The Web: Your Digital Domain 21
    Claiming Education Technology 22
    The Templated Self 26
    Students: Subjects or Objects of Ed-Tech? 27
    Claiming Your Life Bits 28

    Hosting Life Bits 30

    Personal Data Repositories. 32

Chapter 3: Controlling Our Own Technologies 33

    The Indie Web and Edupunk 37

    A Domain of One's Own 40

    Domains and the Democratization of Knowledge 41

Conclusion 45

    Beyond the Portfolio 47

    Claim Is a Verb 49

Appendix 51

    Definitions 51

    Resources 52

References and Resources 55

About the Author

Audrey Watters is a writer who focuses on education technology—the relationship between politics, pedagogy, business, culture, and ed-tech. Although she was two chapters into her PhD dissertation, she decided to abandon academia, and she now happily fulfills the one job recommended to her by a junior high aptitude test—freelance writer.

Audrey has written for *The Atlantic*, *Edutopia*, *MindShift*, *Inside Higher Ed*, *The School Library Journal*, *The Huffington Post*, and elsewhere online and in print. Her work can be found on her website hackeducation.com. She is also the author of *The Monsters of Education Technology*, a collection of public talks and keynotes that she has delivered.

A self-described serial dropout, Audrey did not complete her bachelor's degree at The Johns Hopkins University, nor did she complete her PhD at the University of Oregon. She regularly signs up for massive open online courses (MOOCs) that she does not complete. She does, however, hold a master's degree in folklore from the University of Oregon.

Preface

By Will Richardson

In the 1960s and 1970s, Penguin published a series of what it called *education specials*, short books from a variety of authors such as Neil Postman, Ivan Illich, Herb Kohl, Paulo Freire, Jonathan Kozol, and others. All told, there were more than a dozen works, and they were primarily edgy, provocative essays meant to articulate an acute dissatisfaction with the function of schools at the time. The titles reflected that and included books such as *The Underachieving School*, *Compulsory Mis-Education and the Community of Scholars*, *Teaching as a Subversive Activity*, *Deschooling Society*, and *School Is Dead*, to name a few. Obviously, the messages of these books were not subtle.

Progressive by nature, the authors generally saw their schools as unequal, undemocratic, and controlling places of conformity and indoctrination. They argued, mostly to nonlistening ears, that traditional school narratives were leaving their learners disengaged and lacking in creativity and curiosity, and the systems and structures of schools were deepening instead of ameliorating the inequities in society. A number of the authors argued that universal schooling was a pipe dream from both economic and political perspectives, and schools, if they were to remain, needed to be rethought from the ground up.

Reading many of these works now, it's hard not to be struck by how precisely they describe many of the realities of today's world. It's inarguable that an education in the United States (and elsewhere) remains vastly unequal among socioeconomic groups and various races and ethnicities. The systems that drove schools years ago prevail and, in many cases, are less and less economically viable by the day. By and large, education is something still organized, controlled, and delivered by the institution; very little agency or autonomy is afforded to the learner over his or her own learning. Decades of reform efforts guided principally by politicians and businesspeople have failed to enact the types of widespread changes that those Penguin authors and many others felt were needed for schools to serve every learner equally and adequately in preparing him or her for the world that lies ahead.

It's the "world that lies ahead" that is the focus of this book, part of the *Solutions for Modern Learning* series. Let us say up front that we in no way assume that these books will match the intellectual heft of those writers in the Penguin series (though we hope to come close). However, we aspire to reignite or perhaps even start some important conversations about change in schools, given the continuing longstanding challenges from decades past as well as the modern contexts of a highly networked, technology-packed, fast-changing world whose future looks less predictable by the minute.

Changes in technology since the early 1990s, and specifically, the Internet, have had an enormous impact on how we communicate, create, and most importantly, learn. Nowhere have those effects been felt more acutely than with our learners, most of whom have never known a world without the Internet. In almost all areas of life, in almost every institution and society, the effects of ubiquitously connected technologies we now carry with us in our backpacks and back pockets have been profound, creating amazing opportunities and complex challenges, both of which have been hard to foresee. In no uncertain terms, the world has changed and continues to change quickly and drastically.

Yet, education has remained fairly steadfast, pushing potentially transformative learning devices and programs to the edges, never allowing them to penetrate to the core of learning in schools. Learning in schools looks, sounds, and feels pretty much like it did in the 1970s, if not in the early 1900s.

Here's the problem: increasingly, for those who have the benefit of technology devices and access to the Internet, learning outside of school is more profound, relevant, and long lasting than learning inside the classroom. Connected learners of all ages have agency and autonomy that are stripped from them as they enter school. In a learning context, this is no longer the world that schools were built for, and in that light, it's a pretty good bet that a fundamental redefinition of school is imminent.

While some would like to see schools done away with completely, we believe schools can play a crucially important role in the lives of our youth, the fabric of our communities, and the functioning of our nations. But moving forward, we believe schools can only play these roles if we fully understand and embrace the new contexts that the modern world offers for learning and education. This is not just about equal access to technology and the Internet, although that's a good start. This is about seeing our purpose and our practice through a different lens that understands the new literacies, skills, and dispositions that students need to flourish in a networked world. Our hope is that the books in the *Solutions for Modern Learning* series make that lens clearer and more widespread.

Introduction:
The Manila Envelope

A couple of years ago, my mother gave me a large manila envelope full of my old schoolwork, including drawings, writings, and photos from as far back as preschool. I remembered making some projects, but many I didn't recall. Mostly the envelope contained various administrative records—my report cards, various certificates of achievement, and some ribbons.

My mother, I should note, has always been fastidious about our family's recordkeeping. She saved almost everything, certainly much more than was in the envelope that she eventually gave to me. She stored boxes and boxes of papers in the basement, and she kept a closet full of scrapbooks that chronicled our family vacations and holidays in detail—my childhood as told through photographs, postcards, and travel brochures.

When my parents divorced, an awful disassembling and re-sorting of these scrapbooks took place, as my mother decided what would be hers to keep, what would be my dad's, what would be my brother's, and what would be mine. These were the records of our lives.

That manila envelope my mother gave me was a careful curation of what counts as my education records. They were only a small part of all the schoolwork she'd kept—all those piles of paper that, in a predigital age at least, I'd bring home at the end of every school year (or when commanded to clean out my desk or my locker). The manila envelope didn't include every worksheet and quiz. My mom only kept, and in turn gave to me, what was *meaningful* to her. But these items were also a reflection of the meaningful work that I'd done in school. This was one of those moments of clarity: of all the work I'd done in school, only a fraction was *meaningful* work.

What happens now that schoolwork is increasingly digital (that is, schoolwork that isn't paperwork but has been digitized as work done directly on computers)? Is there a digital equivalent to my manila envelope? Schoolwork done on computers should prompt other questions too, such as: What counts as student work? Content? Data? What happens to that work, not just at the end of the school year but on a day-to-day basis?

Sadly, despite the great promise of technology to transform how we teach and learn, students continue to do menial, repetitive work in new digital worksheets and in new digital environments. One might not see this work as worth preserving in a virtual manila envelope, but it's still worth asking what happens to it. Are schools using the data for decision-making purposes? Are ed-tech companies using the data to build and refine their applications and algorithms? Do students or parents have any say about what happens to these data?

Are students able to retain control or retain a copy of their work? That is, once students work on software at school and not on paper, can they obtain their work to take home or store on their own devices? Can they obtain that work in a format that's actually readable by humans and machines and that's moveable, storable, and sharable as they or their parents deem fit?

Where Is the Digital Manila Envelope?

A couple of years ago, I met a young girl whose school was piloting a one-to-one iPad program. This girl's family wasn't particularly tech oriented, and they didn't have a computer at home. At the beginning of the year when the school offered them a chance to

Introduction: The Manila Envelope

buy the iPad, they declined. It was expensive. They didn't see the point. But by the end of the school year, they had changed their minds—the iPad was easy to use, and their daughter loved it. She downloaded several applications and used them to create a multitude of drawings and write several stories. So, the family approached the school about buying the iPad. But it was too late, the school told them. The purchasing opportunity was limited to the beginning of the year. Therefore, the family was required to return the iPad with all of their daughter's schoolwork, drawings, stories, and data on it. There was no manila envelope—physical or digital—for much of her sixth-grade schoolwork.

The family had no home iTunes account to sync with the girl's iPad data—that's what you're supposed to do to get your data off of an iPad, school issued or otherwise. You sync the data to your personal computer at home. There are a lot of assumptions in this scenario—about access, equipment, and the home.

Even if students do have computers at home, schools often create "dummy" accounts for the devices they issue to students and for the software they require students to use. That means, even if students *do* have their own computers or iTunes accounts at home, it doesn't matter. Their school-issued devices often are registered to "student25@school.com" or some other fabricated email account. That means the data likely doesn't sync. Perhaps the data can be exported, but it often cannot be accessed; it cannot be reconciled with preexisting accounts. There is no digital manila envelope.

This isn't just about flaws in Apple devices, of course. It isn't simply about how hardware and software are administered at school. We must ask a broader question: is there a safe digital place—*any* safe place—where learners can store their schoolwork and school records, not just for the duration of a course or for the length of school year, but for posterity?

Are we providing learners with those safe and secure digital places? If not, why not? And if they don't exist, can we build them? Can we build a digital manila envelope? What would it look like? How would it function? These are questions worth considering, especially more than educators, administrators, parents, and students currently do as we compel and often require people to use technology in schools and in the workplace.

We must consider what student data are being created, what student data are being collected (and by whom), how to protect that data, and how to preserve it. Furthermore, we must put the control of that data into the hands of the students themselves, in no small part because learning now happens beyond school walls (and school software)—at home and on the go, thanks to mobile devices.

My mother wanted to preserve my schoolwork for posterity. *Posterity*—that word sounds a lot like *Posterous*. Posterous was a microblogging platform founded in 2008 and acquired by Twitter in 2012. Shortly afterward, it shut down. Users had the opportunity to download their data, and the Internet archive made a valiant attempt to preserve all the sites. Posterous was a free tool that many students, educators, librarians, and others used to share and store writing, photos, video, and other digital content. The closure of Posterous was hardly the first or the only time something like this happened to a digital tool—free or paid—that's been popular for educational purposes. Schools often demand that students put their work into a learning management system (LMS), for example, where they lose access to it at the end of the semester or when they graduate. And for that flawed functionality, schools spend hundreds of thousands of dollars.

This is a reminder of how fragile our digital records might be. We've long been cautioned in school that "this will go down on your permanent record." But now we exist at this strange juncture in which our school records are both much more permanent and much less so. We pour ourselves—our thoughts and ideas—into one application or another, and then these applications go offline. The company is sold or acquired, and our data are sold along with it.

Increasingly, we do not have the ability to look at our permanent records. We cannot access them or correct them. The data we've created in various digital learning environments is not ours to examine, let alone dictate who else might be able to view it. Can teachers access it? Administrators? Software engineers? Marketers?

So, when we demand a safe digital place to store student data, or their permanent records, it means a couple of things. The safety of data must include both permanence and privacy. That is, student data must preserved, and it must be under student control. (Students should have the option to hit the Delete button.)

Creating the Digital Manila Envelope

I want you to imagine what a digital manila envelope might contain. Grades? Test scores? Attendance records? That's the stuff of traditional, analog education records. However, technologies are reshaping those records as we create massive amounts of data and metadata (or *big data*).

A digital manila envelope should be more than just storage for virtual report cards. What about the pictures a child draws in preschool and kindergarten? What about the poems, essays, and book reports he or she writes? Why not keep everything? After all, digital storage is cheap! This might include a list of every book checked out from the library, along with all the highlights from those books and notes in the margins. It might include titles of every educational video watched, along with the metadata from the viewing—all the pauses, rewinds, and fast forwards; all the comments on discussion forums and all the status updates; all that data a student might create thanks to computer technologies. This might include every single mouse click on every single piece of software, whether it's school issued or required, whether it's formally ed-tech or not. Suddenly, this digital manila envelope starts to sound a little invasive, particularly if someone other than the student has control over the data and the profile.

Daphne Koller, cofounder of the online education startup Coursera, explains that the benefits of this site go far beyond offering a myriad of interesting classes to the general public. "By collecting every click, homework submission, quiz, and forum note from tens of thousands of students," online education sites like Coursera have become "a data mine that offers a new way to study learning" (May, 2012).

In Coursera, do students own their own data? Can they study it? Can they control with whom it's shared? What are the risks of someone other than the student amassing all these data? Can a student export his or her data from Coursera, for example, into a personal digital manila envelope? In Coursera and almost all education software, the current answer to these questions is *no*. The data do not belong to students, and students can't access them. Again, there is no digital manila envelope.

Claiming Education Technology

This book aims to tell a different story about students' digital work, content, and data in an attempt to build a different future for education technologies. My goal is to identify ways to help preserve and protect student data and, just as importantly student identity—or at the very least, prompt you to ask questions about what kinds of technologies that would require.

Collecting student data shouldn't merely consist of assessing students based on school goals and needs. Student data reflect student identity. As such, we must consider how we can put students in control of their schoolwork, content, and data. We must do more to support students' control of their learning as well. That's not simply a technological problem, of course.

How do we build education technologies that enable students to control their schoolwork, content, and data? What does that control look like technologically, pedagogically, and administratively? How do we make sure students have a digital manila envelope?

Introduction: The Manila Envelope

The title of this book is *Claim Your Domain*. It's a nod in part to the Domain of One's Own initiative (http://umw.domains) out of the University of Mary Washington (UMW). (You will read more about this initiative in chapter 3.) The Domain of One's Own project gives every student and staff member his or her own domain. It isn't simply web space on the university servers—an .edu with a slash tilde namespace. The initiative gives students and staff members their *own* personal domains located at their *own* chosen URLs, for example: www.whatever-they-want.com. The university pays for domain registration and hosting while students are enrolled. When students graduate, the domain and the data go with them. It's theirs—their own domains.

This book stresses that the word *domain* matters—a digital home. Students should have their *own* space on the web, a space for a blog or multiple blogs. They should have a digital portfolio for their academic work that can become a professional portfolio if they so choose—a place to store their digital material in the cloud—their own manila envelope.

The word *claim* matters too. We've let students' digital data go elsewhere for a while now. We have built systems in which students' digital data are not under their control. Students do not have a say in what happens to their data or who has access to them. They do not have a say in storage or sharing. They do not control their data as users of computers and certainly not as learners.

To *claim your domain* means just that: put students in control of their schoolwork, content, and data. Put them in charge of their learning as well as the demonstration of that learning.

Chapter Overview

The information in this book attempts to claim education technology and, more importantly, to claim learning for learners themselves.

Chapter 1 looks at the state of learners' digital domains today. This chapter explores what it means now that more and more schoolwork is digital. It attempts to answer the questions: What student data are being collected? What happens to those data? Who owns those data?

Chapter 2 examines alternatives to the current state of education technology. It looks at the current technological alternatives as well as those that have been imagined by authors of another era, those who want to see a more progressive and learner-centered world. It also provides some practical strategies for claiming your domain, at least as much as you can within today's education technology.

Chapter 3 asks what education and other technologies—that learners can actually control for themselves—could and should look like (philosophically as well as technologically). What must we demand of students and parents in terms of data literacy and computer literacy if we plan on turning over these efforts to them? Claiming a learner's domain is incredibly powerful and radical and, admittedly, very ambitious. There is much in both the current state of education and education technology that stands in the way of these efforts. But that doesn't mean we shouldn't try.

My mother gave me a manila envelope full of *some* of the work I'd done as a K–12 student. It was her collection and curation of my work. It's hard for me to challenge her role as the curator and collector. I recognize that not everyone has a mom like mine. Nonetheless, I recognize the power of curation and collection. And I want us to think about what that means as we move from paper to digital.

How do we make sure that students control their work? How do we make sure their work persists? How do we make sure they have a say about who can see and share it? Sharing is an important feature unlocked by digital technologies. Unlike a manila envelope full of papers—the one my mother gave me is now tucked away in my closet, I confess—a digital envelope is more easily accessible, duplicable, durable, and sharable.

Chapter 1
The Learner's Digital Domain

In the third century BC, the Library of Alexandria was tasked with collecting all the world's knowledge, storing a copy of every written work in scroll and book form. Of course, papyrus isn't particularly durable, as the infamous burning of the library unfortunately demonstrated. Even without fire, paper records are precariously fragile and temporary.

Now that so much of our writing and recordkeeping are digital, we might presume that all the world's knowledge is safe from loss or destruction. You'll often hear people say that the Internet is forever. Once you post something online, it never goes away. And while it's true that making copies no longer requires labor-intensive transcription or paper-intensive reprinting, we face new challenges. The Internet isn't forever. Certainly technologies become obsolete. Websites go away. Links "rot," sometimes faster than paper does.

The preservation of digital materials requires us to think differently about storage, in part because of the ever-changing formats in which we store data—Word documents, WordPerfect documents, Google Docs, PDFs, Rich Text Format—which of these will be around and legible thousands of years from now?

We must rethink storage too, because the amount of that digital material we are tasked with preserving is skyrocketing. All of the Library of Alexandria—about 500,000 scrolls—could fit onto a single USB drive today. In 2012, IBM (n.d.) estimated that the digital universe contains 2.5 quintillion bytes of data. No doubt, that number has continued to grow exponentially since then. It's hard for people to fathom a number that big; it's also hard to fathom that the contents of the Library of Alexandria can now fit in your pocket.

Much of this explosion of newly created data comes from sensors and nonhuman sources. However, each of us is doing our part to create massive amounts of data. IBM (n.d.) claims that 90 percent of the world's data has been created since 2010. Every minute, one hundred hours of video are uploaded to YouTube and more than 350,000 tweets are sent. Google processes about 3.5 billion searches per day. Facebook gets about 4.5 billion "likes" per day. According to the *MIT Technology Review* (Tucker, 2013):

> A typical American office worker produces 1.8 million megabytes of data each year. That is about 5,000 megabytes a day, including downloaded movies, Word files, email, and the bits generated by computers as that information is moved along mobile networks or across the Internet.

If the typical office worker creates that much data, how much does the typical student generate? And just as important, what happens to those data? Are they stored safely and securely? Do students recognize that they are the source of so much digital data? Do they have any say about what happens to that information?

What does "all the world's knowledge" look like today, and how do student data interact with that? Thanks to Internet technology, students can conceivably contribute to and build the world's knowledge. Unfortunately, the education technologies that are commonly used in schools rarely give students the opportunity to do that.

What Data "Count" as Education Records?

The term *student data* might sound incongruent with *all the world's knowledge*. Student data and schoolwork are still often seen as the banality of someone's official school records. Too often, student work is seen as, even designed to be, menial but not meaningful. Thanks to new technologies, our notion of student data is expanding, and if we rethink some of our education practices as well, we can certainly help connect students' work to the rest of the world. This means we have to think more critically and expansively about what counts as student data and what counts as someone's official education records.

This matters because official education records afford students all kinds of legal protections surrounding the storage and privacy—and ideally, the security—of that information. These protections dictate, for example, who gets to look at student data. They specify who gets to correct data. Ostensibly, at least, they define who is responsible for the security and privacy of data, such as the school, the parent, the technology company, or even the student.

But what actually counts as official education records? Unfortunately, the answer is vague at best. The United States Department of Education (n.d.) defines education records as follows: "Education records are those records that are directly related to a student and are maintained by an educational agency or institution or by a party acting for the agency or institution." That doesn't offer much precision about what "those records" might be.

In practice, it's mostly left to states, districts, and schools to interpret what counts. Often, what counts remains a pretty traditional notion of student records: name, address, grade, some demographic data, and so on. That is to say, it doesn't include all the additional data that students now generate because so much of their work happens via computer technologies. And that means a lot of data are not protected by the meager laws that specify what can happen to official education records. What happens to those data is often delineated by the contracts that schools sign with various software and hardware vendors. It's outlined in the terms of service of those contracts—terms that students rarely read or understand.

This should prompt us to ask, "For what exact data are schools and other education-related institutions stewards? Is it only what appears on students' transcripts, such as dates of attendance and final course grades?"

What other information might we want to include in a student's official education records? How about library checkouts, gym visits, and sports records? Cafeteria and bookstore purchases? Minutes from student meetings? Trips to the nurse and the guidance counselor? Times in and out of the dormitory? Locations on and off the school bus? What about *all* the data that are being collected and generated by students?

I should emphasize here that when I say *data*, I don't just mean numbers. Essays, photos, and videos are data too. What about students' search engine history and their "likes" and tweets? Their LMS logins and durations of their LMS sessions? Blog and forum comment history? Internet usage while on campus? Emails sent and received? Chat logs? Pages read in digital textbooks? Videos watched on Khan Academy, along with if and where they paused? Exercises completed on that platform? Wikipedia visits? Wikipedia edits? Time spent and tasks accomplished in Minecraft? Keystrokes and mouse clicks?

Keystrokes and mouse clicks, along with biometric data, is how more and more education companies say they plan to confirm students' identities as they move through various assessment platforms. It's how more and more schools plan to monitor students as well. That means that all these data gathered about students will be used in some pretty powerful ways. And it's probably worth noting that unlike changing passwords, changing grades, growing, or learning, biometric data cannot be changed.

When we talk about student data, we must think about much more than the official transcript in its analog sense. Student data is all of that to be sure: the student's grade level and grades, how often he or she attends and misses class, and what he or she scores on various assessments. However, *student data* usually refers to a huge amount of information well beyond test scores and report cards. Some of this is new information that schools probably haven't considered—that is, they haven't thought about the implications of the data capture or data analysis and storage (although the providers of education technology software typically have).

Some schools have considered collecting data, and for reasons that coincide with other school practices—to monitor, surveil, and control —students are on course to fulfill the school's goals. Quite likely, no matter what schools do or how little or how much they decide to collect, it's certain that they gather a huge amount of information that students aren't even aware that they're generating.

Why Education Data Matter

One of the promises of all these education data is that, when collected and analyzed, they will reveal new insights into how students learn. The ability to glean these insights from student data is the cornerstone of the emerging field of learning analytics. *Learning analytics* involves using student data to more accurately identify what students understand and don't understand, which students are at risk of failing and dropping out, and so on. In turn, new software will be developed to move students more efficiently through the education system. Students will be able to move at their own pace because the software "understands" each individual student's educational needs and strengths. All of this is predicated on the notion that learning can be measured. This means that the data analyzed are certain types of data—the most easily quantifiable.

It's worth noting, however, that there are many obstacles to making use of the data that schools collect about students. Some of these obstacles are technical; some are policy related; some are pedagogical; some are cultural; some are scientific; some are ethical; and some are intertwined with our perceptions about privacy and technology and our expectations of what teaching and learning should look like.

For starters, not all education software "talks" with other education software. The data in one software system are often trapped there. Once you enter the data, you can't get them out again, at least not in a format that other software can utilize or not without a lot of manual data entry. But more important perhaps, the data that are tracked by school software often meet the needs of administrators and educators but not the students themselves. Schools go to great lengths to record data about student attendance, for example. They're legally compelled to do so. However, they don't bother to make note of students' interests. Schools might collect all sorts of data about students, but these are not necessarily data that can offer much insight into who students are, let alone who they might become.

Again, students often aren't aware of what data are being collected about them. They rarely have the opportunity to consent to data collection or data analysis, nor do they have the opportunity to request a copy of these data for themselves. That means we have a responsibility to help students understand the data they generate and to ask on behalf of all learners: "What data are being collected? What data are being stored and for how long? What data are being shared and with whom?"

Who Owns Student Data?

And that brings us to two of the most important questions to ask about student data: "Who owns the data?" and "Who controls all the data?"

Even though laws like the United States' Family Educational Rights and Privacy Act (FERPA) (United States Department of Education, n.d.) claim to protect the privacy of students' education records, there isn't a clear provision stating that student records belong *to the student*. That particular law, first passed in 1974, doesn't do a good job of recognizing how much student records have changed since the 1980s, thanks to computers. Furthermore, recent revisions to FERPA have made it easier for schools—the guardians or stewards of those student records—to release student data to companies that provide educational services and software (for example, the LMS, adaptive learning software, digital textbook publisher, online course provider, and the cafeteria point-of-sale system). As long as these companies offer services that fulfill "educational purposes," data sharing is legal.

It's not really clear what an *educational purpose* means when it comes to who can access student data. This doesn't necessarily mean that the data sharing is nefarious. However, students never have any input about this process.

The question of who owns student data is further complicated by the fact that FERPA's protections—as out-of-date and as frustrating as they have become in a digital world—only cover students in formal academic settings. That seems particularly noteworthy since so much learning now happens outside school via YouTube, blogs, Wikipedia, video games, and so on. In addition, FERPA protections only cover students enrolled in programs that receive federal funds under certain Department of Education programs (United States Department of Education, n.d.). That leaves open a whole swath of companies—many new for-profits in the education technology sector, for example—that need make no pretense of protecting student data under this particular regulation.

The following is part of the privacy policy from the World Education University (n.d.), which offers online courses for free: "WEU may share your information with any third party outside of our organization as necessary to underwrite free educational offerings.

WEU may contact you about specials, new products or services, or changes to this privacy policy."

Most people don't fully read through the terms of service of any given software program. I'm guessing that very few students think through the ways in which their personal data can be used by products and services associated with their schooling or in which their intellectual property might be assigned to someone other than themselves. Few students get to read the terms of service, particularly for tools they're required to use in school. And few teachers or schools even think about this issue. We trust education, and we trust education technology—often uncritically.

Students usually don't consider the security and safety of their data, whether they are in an ad-supported education program like WEU, a venture capitalist-backed education program like Coursera, an endowment-rich school like the University of Columbia, or in a public or private school at the K–12 level.

What happens to student data? "I don't know." We shrug. How long will they be stored? "I don't know." We shrug again. Who has access? "I don't know." We shrug yet again. "But hey, this new ed-tech tool is free!" teachers say. And usually that is enough.

Technology writer Douglas Rushkoff argues that if you're not paying for the product, you *are* the product (Solon, 2011). I think it's actually far more complicated and far more insidious than that. When it comes to our metadata, it seems we're becoming the product whether we pay for the service or not. Students are the product of the LMS, for example, even though schools spend hundreds of thousands of dollars every year on contracts with LMS companies. Of course, when it comes to schooling, we're already well accustomed to talking about students as the product of the system—heads to fill with information, lives to shape, and now, thanks to computers, metadata to mine.

Education faces some huge questions when it comes data generation. What happens to these data? What will be the role of the algorithm in education, for example? How will *big data*—the massive amounts of data we are currently gathering—and learning analytics shape the decisions we make in the classroom, in institutions, and as students, professors, administrators, and parents? How will an obsession with data shape our priorities and cause us to pay attention to certain signals, such as test scores, and ignore others? And, most important, what really happens to all that student data?

Can we create a digital manila envelope? Is there a way for students to extract or control their education records—not just in their traditional meaning but in their expanded meaning, now that we know we have all these data about learners? What would this envelope look like? What do we want this envelope to do to protect student data in terms of privacy and security? Do we want this envelope to reinforce the idea that student data should be tracked and measured to reveal something about learning, or do we want to actually subvert these practices so students themselves have a say in how their data are collected, stored, and used?

Claiming Student Data

If we recognize that all of us are generating thousands of megabytes of data every day as users of the Internet and as workers, then we must stop to consider what that means for students who (let's be honest) are also users and workers in this new digital world. What does it mean to expose student work to algorithms? How do the judgments of algorithms differ from the judgments of teachers? Does it matter? I would insist that yes, it does. It's important for educators to recognize the power of data, and I think it's educators' responsibility, in turn, to help students understand what happens to their work—*all* the data that they produce as students and users of the Internet.

It's important to recognize that with all this data creation and collection, student work isn't simply the kinds of worksheets and assignments that quickly get tossed away or maybe constitute a blip in the gradebook. Those data, while seemingly meaningless for teachers, parents, and students, are incredibly valuable for companies collecting data at scale and building algorithms.

If we find this practice to be exploitative or controlling, what are our alternatives? What might that mean in terms of school policy? What might that mean in terms of school technology? It's possible and perhaps even imperative that we all learn to control our own data and claim our digital lives. We must at least begin to formulate good questions to ask so that there is informed consent when we use education technologies.

What do we want students to do or be in a digital world? If nothing else, they should have agency, autonomy, and critical awareness of what it means to live, work, and play in a digital world. That means we want them to have their own spaces, their own voices, and their own domains. That's why this book is titled *Claim Your Domain*—we need to build education technologies that claim students' content and data.

That requires both a theory and a practice—an articulation of why it matters that students own their domains and why it matters that we help think through and build out those technologies now, even if our leaders and learners aren't necessarily ready.

Chapter 2
Why Claim Your Domain?

One of the most powerful learning technologies humans have ever created is the World Wide Web. Its power doesn't lie simply in all the *content*—a modern version of the Library of Alexandria that contains all the world's knowledge. We get too distracted by that. The power of the web lies mostly in human connections, the intellectual and social networks that we build.

The fact that schools block and filter the web and discourage its use is a shame. If schools fail to help students learn about how the web works and how it will likely form some aspect of their digital identity, it is a terrible missed opportunity.

In 2010, *Wired Magazine* tried to argue that the web is dead. Then-editor Chris Anderson and columnist Michael Wolff (2010) write:

> As much as we love the open, unfettered web, we're abandoning it for simpler, sleeker services that just work. . . . Over the past few years, one of the most important shifts in the digital world has been the move from the wide-open web to semiclosed platforms that use the Internet for transport but not the browser for display.

Although billions of pages are on the web, the majority of traffic flows to giant sites like Facebook. And these sites, much like earlier Internet portals like America Online (AOL) and Prodigy, discourage users from venturing elsewhere. Furthermore, much of the most popular and trafficked applications—for example, video games and video streaming—aren't accessed via a web browser. A move away from the "wide-open web" to these closed, proprietary platforms would mean, in turn, that some of the benefits of the web, such as linking to resources and accessibility, are in peril. And this could have major implications, again, for how and where our personal data flow.

But reports of the web's death are greatly exaggerated. Indeed, despite the interests of many technology companies in funneling our activities into applications that are closed off from the web—without URLs, syndication, data portability, and often without privacy protections in which all our activities are set to be data mined—the web remains. It remains a site of great hope and great promise. It remains easily readable, writable, programmable, designable, and hackable. (I mean this last feature as a strength, not a danger.)

And despite the efforts of Facebook and other big technology silos of the world, there's a push for a return to the web—the *Indie web*, as some describe it. This is the web that many of us fell in love with when we first dialed up and escaped to AOL. I'll talk more about the Indie web in the next chapter, but this desire to return to and protect the web recognizes that there's something important about the ability for anyone to participate in this new online platform as a writer, not just a reader, and as a builder, not just a buyer. The Indie web can be viewed much like "indie" bookstores and "indie" record stores. We recognize that it is important to support alternatives to major corporate creators and sellers of media.

Media—that is, the content we create—is important, even critical, to the development of our identities as well as the development and protection of our well-being. Increasingly, we recognize that our identities are not secure in the hands of startups or big corporations—these companies go away. They are not secure in the hands of schools either. Schools are not in the business of long-term data storage, and they increasingly outsource their IT to those very start-ups and big corporations.

We must become the holders of our own data, but not so that we hide it away from view—to store it, as my mother did, in unopened boxes in the basement. We should share it with others. But we should be able to do so on our own terms and on our own domains.

The Web: Your Digital Domain

Claim your domain—that phrase requires some explanation. Let's start with what we mean by domain. The word can have many meanings. *Domain* is a territory controlled by a state or government. It can refer to a specific sphere of knowledge. It also means home. It means a space on the Internet marked by a specific address and controlled by an individual or organization.

Home. Territory. Space. Place. To claim your domain online—and specifically, to help learners claim their domains—taps into all of these meanings. It is about taking control over our virtual spaces and our personal, virtual territory. It is about knowledge—our personal knowledge that we can showcase to others. It is about building a digital home.

Domain is also a specific technological construct, a core part of the World Wide Web. A domain name is an address on the web, representing a particular Internet protocol (IP) resource, such as a computer or a server connected to the Internet. A uniform resource locator or URL—the string we type into the address bar on a web browser—points you to a domain.

The architecture of this web-specific domain is important, as Trevor Owens (2014) points out in his book *Designing Online Communities*:

> At the most fundamental level, the designs of the web operate on a set of protocols. The TCP/IP (Telecommunications Control Protocol / Internet Protocol) and the DNS (Domain Names System) are the fundamental

> protocols that enable the web to establish structures of control. . . . Many continue to see the web as a platform that emancipates users to create and share their ideas and build collective knowledge and intelligence, but that system is highly structured and designed to record and track users in the way the system's most basic protocols function. (p. 10)

Domains are, as Owens notes, part of the World Wide Web's infrastructure of control, just as they are promised to be instruments of our freedom. What is popularly known as Kranzberg's Law reminds us that technology is neither good nor bad, nor is it neutral (Kranzberg, 1986). Built into the web's very core, we have tracking mechanisms—something that proponents of web-based technologies in schools, let alone much of society, haven't really confronted. But we also have a very powerful way to rethink domain—knowledge, space, and systems of control—particularly if we put the management of personal data and websites into the hands of students.

Domains are addresses to virtual places. Domains can be purchased (or, more accurately, leased) from domain name registrars. (You can find more information about this in the Resources section of the appendix on page 51.) And that means you can and should own your own domain. I own audreywatters.com, for example, and I bought my son his name as a domain too.

You should be in control of your virtual place and your digital portfolio. After all, it is your work, your identity, and your data. You should be able to build that portfolio and decorate your place as you see fit. That means you get to decide what to save and what to share.

Claiming Education Technology

Technology entrepreneur and writer Anil Dash (2012b) writes a lament in "The Web We Lost." Unlike the prediction in *Wired* magazine (Anderson & Wolff, 2010) that we are all happily moving away from the web and into apps, Dash expresses nostalgia for earlier days, noting features we have moved away from to our detriment.

> In the early days of the social web, there was a broad expectation that regular people might own their own identities by having their own websites, instead of being dependent on a few big sites to host their online identity. In this vision, you would own your own domain name and have complete control over its contents, rather than having a handle tacked on to the end of a huge company's site. This was a sensible reaction to the realization that big sites rise and fall in popularity, but that regular people need an identity that persists longer than those sites do.

Dash (2012a) follows up this article with "Rebuilding the Web We Lost," in which he outlines some of the steps we can take to return to a web that values public spaces over profits and respects privacy and usability. "Explore architectural changes," Dash (2012a) suggests. Rethink who should build and can build our technologies (currently, he explains, they are "a narrow band of privileged graduates from a small number of top-tier schools, overwhelmingly male and focused narrowly on the traditional Silicon Valley geography.") Challenge the current funding model. To do so—on a small or grand scale—seems incredibly important for the future of the web but also for the future of education technology.

In addition to the verb *rebuild* that Dash uses, I like to use the verb *claim*. It's a nod to taking back and owning power, agency, and control, something that is absolutely necessary when we talk about students' learning experiences and their work, content, and data. But I also invoke the word *claim* with a nod to both the ecological and political implications of the word. We describe the web as a system that connects people—a technological ecosystem. The fact that we must *claim* the web and, more broadly, education technology should remind us of the damage that has been done to this ecosystem and the damage that might still occur, specifically by viewing technology users as resources to be mined. More and more, it seems that technologies are designed to serve as some sort of an extraction effort, with all the emphasis on the value in individuals' data to companies (but not on the individuals themselves).

"Data is the new oil," headlines proclaim (Palmer, 2006). "Data is just like crude," one market analyst states. "It's valuable, but if unrefined it cannot really be used. It has to be changed into gas, plastic, chemicals, etc., to create a valuable entity that drives profitable activity; so must data be broken down, analyzed for it to have value" (as cited in Palmer, 2006). And if data is "the new oil," then it must be mined.

The term *data mining* is actually quite new—less than twenty-five years old at the writing of this book. Certainly, statistics, algorithms, pattern recognition, and the analyses based on these have a much longer history. In the 1960s, statisticians referred to pouring through data without an a priori hypothesis as *data dredging*, a practice that carried a negative connotation. It was in roughly this same time period that the United States saw the passing of new laws—several of which, like FERPA, are still on the books—that sought to address some of the growing concerns about data and their potential misuse as banking, health care, and government services became increasingly computerized.

Data dredging and *data mining* are technological processes, but they also are very powerful metaphors. *Data dredging* conjures the image of searching or excavating a large, fluid pool of information—dredging up information from the bottom of the pool, information that's been buried and otherwise inaccessible. Despite the importance or value in what's being harvested, dredging in the physical world is largely recognized as disturbing the ecosystem and leaving behind toxic chemicals. *Data mining* suggests a more targeted resource extraction. It certainly suggests a more lucrative one. But the potential for grave damage to the environment continues.

To call data "the new oil" is particularly resonant in our currently energy-hungry and fossil fuel-reliant economy. And for what it's worth, some data scientists have pushed back on the oil metaphor—or at least some of the uncritical glee surrounding its usage—to simply talk about the potential for profits. Jer Thorp (2012), an educator and the former data artist in residence at *The New York Times*, suggests that the *data is the new oil* metaphor requires a critical eye. Data aren't just lying beneath the surface waiting to be extracted. Thorp writes:

> Perhaps the "data as oil" idea can foster some much-needed criticality. Our experience with oil has been fraught; fortunes made have been balanced with dwindling resources, bloody mercenary conflicts, and a terrifying climate crisis. If we are indeed making the first steps into economic terrain that will be as transformative (and possibly as risky) as that of the petroleum industry, foresight will be key. We have already seen "data spills" happen (when large amounts of personal data are inadvertently leaked). Will it be much longer until we see dangerous data drilling practices? Or until we start to see long-term effects from "data pollution"?
>
> One of the places where we'll have to tread most carefully—another place where our data/oil model can be useful—is in the realm of personal data. A great deal of the profit that is being made right now in the data world is being made through the use of human-generated information. Our browsing habits, our conversations with friends, our movements and location—all of these things are being monetized. This is deeply human data, though very often it is not treated as such. Here, perhaps we can invoke a comparison to fossil fuel in a useful way: where oil is composed of the compressed bodies of long-dead microorganisms, this personal data is made from the compressed fragments of our personal lives. It is a dense condensate of our human experience.

If we are to embrace the *new oil* metaphor, Thorp insists that we do so critically, thinking through all the implications, not merely those that have the "mining" executives rubbing their hands together in glee, anticipating the profits they will make.

The Templated Self

Many software packages promise personalization, but in reality, they present a very restricted set of choices of who you can be and how you can interact, both with your own data and content and with other people. Gender, for example, is often a drop-down menu where you can choose either male or female, ignoring a range of gender identities and expressions. Or, software might ask for a first and last name, which is complicated if you have multiple family names (as some Spanish-speaking people do) or your family name is your first name (as names in China are ordered). Your name is presented in a way the software engineers and designers deem fit: sometimes first name, sometimes title and last name, and typically with a profile picture. Changing your username—after marriage or divorce, for example—is often challenging, if not impossible.

Similarly, you get to interact with others based on processes that the software engineers determined and designed. On Twitter, for example, you cannot direct-message people who do not follow you, and all interactions must be one hundred forty characters or less.

This restriction of the presentation and performance of one's identity online is what cyborg anthropologist Amber Case (2011) calls the *templated self*. She explains this as:

> A self or identity that is produced through various participation architectures, the act of producing a virtual or digital representation of self by filling out a user interface with personal information.
>
> Facebook and Twitter are examples of the templated self. The shape of a space affects how one can move, what one does, and how one interacts with someone else. It also defines how influential and what constraints there are to that identity. A more flexible, but still templated space is WordPress. A hand-built site is much less templated, as one is free to fully create their digital self in any way possible. Those in Second Life play with and modify templated selves

> into increasingly unique online identities. MySpace pages are templates, but the lack of constraints can lead to spaces that are considered irritating to others.

As we spend more and more time and effort developing our identities online, being forced to use preordained templates constrains us rather than allowing us to be anyone or say anything online. This seems particularly important to keep in mind when we think about children's and teens' identity development. How are their identities being templated? While Case's examples point to mostly social technologies, education technologies are also participation architectures. Similarly, they produce and restrict one's digital representation.

Of course, you could argue that the education system is already incredibly interested in templating students, not to mention templating knowledge. We see this in requirements for graduation, courses, essays, discipline, tenure, and so on. Many education technologies loyally reinscribe these into the digital world, developing profiles and algorithms that direct and display school-related accomplishments. The LMS is perhaps the perfect example of this. New adaptive technologies, often connected to textbooks, assessments, and LMSs, are arguably the next wave of tools that seek to produce the *templated learner*. A point of resistance, then, is building and controlling one's own domain.

Students: Subjects or Objects of Ed-Tech?

Part of the problem we face when it comes to rethinking education technologies is that we must also confront the systems and practices already in place in education. Many of them posit students as the objects, not the subjects, of education. That is, these technologies mean to build, conform, fill with knowledge, restrict, constrict, and construct students. Students aren't the subjects; they aren't building and constructing knowledge. They don't get a lot of choices, and they don't get much, if any, control over their learning.

If education technology views students as objects, then that makes it easier for software providers to collect and analyze student data without student permission. If education technology views students as objects, then what students do isn't worthy of much, or so we're told. It's not even worthy of being stored permanently in a manila envelope.

Claiming Your Life Bits

Arguably, part of the problem we face when it comes to rethinking both the web and education technology is the word *data*. It's such a clinical word. To some people, it implies just numbers. It implies the extraneous and unimportant, when in fact the opposite is true. The more data we create, the more of ourselves we reveal—the more bits of our life.

Life bits is a better term than *data* to describe all that we're creating now thanks to new technologies. Using *life bits* instead of *data* might also help to highlight why consolidating and controlling our personal data in our own domains and our own repositories is such an important concept. The term *life bits* might help us to recognize that all this data we're creating—intentionally and unintentionally—are *us*. Life bits represent bits and bytes of data, sure, but also bits and pieces of our lives. Opening up life bits for others to mine sounds a lot less appealing than mining something impersonal like data.

The notion of life bits comes from Microsoft researcher Gordon Bell, who undertook a project starting in 1999 called *MyLifeBits*. This project involved building a personal archive of all the digital assets related to his life and going forward to capture, in close to real time, all the digital data he created (Microsoft Research, 2015). It is, as the website describes the project, "a lifetime store of everything. It is the fulfillment of Vannevar Bush's 1945 memex vision, including full-text search, text and audio annotations, and hyperlinks."

Vannevar Bush (1945), then director of the U.S. Office of Scientific Research and Development, describes the memex—a portmanteau of *memory* and *index*—in an *Atlantic Monthly* article, "As We May Think":

> Consider a future device for individual use, which is a sort of mechanized private file and library. It needs a name, and, to coin one at random, "memex" will do. A memex is a device in which an individual stores all his books, records, and communications, and which is mechanized so that it may be consulted with exceeding speed and flexibility. It is an enlarged intimate supplement to his memory.
>
> It consists of a desk, and while it can presumably be operated from a distance, it is primarily the piece of furniture at which he works. On the top are slanting translucent screens, on which material can be projected for convenient reading. There is a keyboard, and sets of buttons and levers. Otherwise it looks like an ordinary desk.
>
> In one end is the stored material. The matter of bulk is well taken care of by improved microfilm. Only a small part of the interior of the memex is devoted to storage, the rest to mechanism. Yet if the user inserted 5,000 pages of material a day it would take him hundreds of years to fill the repository, so he can be profligate and enter material freely.

Bush's vision for the memex predates the World Wide Web by more than forty years. But we can see here some of its philosophical roots—the idea of having a personal device that is both a library and a record of one's own thoughts (and for our purposes here, one's own learning as well).

Inspired by Bush, Bell's MyLifeBits is an attempt to build a device that can capture and store everything—"a lifetime's worth of articles, books, cards, CDs, letters, memos, papers, photos, pictures, presentations, home movies, videotaped lectures, and voice recordings" (Microsoft Research, 2015). With his colleagues at Microsoft Research, Bell has helped develop software to make all of his data searchable, retrievable, and annotatable. The goal of the project is revealed in the title of Bell's book, *Total Recall*.

Hosting Life Bits

Another former Microsoft researcher, Jon Udell, added the word *hosted* to Bell's concept, arguing that a repository of life bits could be stored in the cloud where it could interact with other repositories and other people—life bits plus the Internet.

In a blog post, Udell (2007) writes:

> Today my digital assets are spread out all over the place. Some are on various websites that I control, and a lot more that I don't. Others are on various local hard disks that I control, and a lot more that I don't. It's become really clear to me that I'd be willing to pay for the service of consolidating all this stuff, syndicating it to wherever it's needed, and guaranteeing its availability throughout—and indeed beyond—my lifetime.
>
> The scenario, as I've been painting it in conversations with friends and associates, begins at childbirth. In addition to a social security number, everyone gets a handle to a chunk of managed storage. How that's coordinated by public- and private-sector entities is an open question, but here's how it plays out from the individual's point of view.

Udell (2007) then imagines what it might mean to collect all of one's important data from grade school, high school, college, and work—and have the ability to turn them into a portfolio—for posterity, personal reflection, and professional display on the web.

> Grade 3
>
> Your teacher assigns a report that will be published in your e-portfolio, which is a website managed by the school. Your parents tell you to write the report, and publish it into your space. Then they release it to the school's content management system. A couple of years later, the school switches to a new system and

> breaks all the old URLs. But the original version remains accessible throughout your parents' lives, and yours, and even your kids'.
>
> Grade 8
>
> On the class trip to Washington, DC, you take a batch of digital photos. You want to share them on MySpace, so you do, but not directly, because MySpace isn't really your space. So you upload the photos to the place that really is your space, where they'll be permanently and reliably available. [T]hen you syndicate them into MySpace for the social effects that happen there.
>
> Grade 11
>
> You're applying to colleges. You publish your essay into your space, then syndicate it to the common application service. The essay points to supporting evidence—your e-portfolio, recommendations—which are also . . . permanently recorded in your space.

The idea of hosted life bits is that we each have the ability—at the very least, access to the technology or to a service—to maintain our own data repository for ourselves but also for our children and families. Parents could manage their children's repositories and then hand over the keys to their children when they're grown. Adults, in turn, could manage their repositories and then hand them over to their children later (or perhaps gift them to an archive or institution).

Udell's invocation of MySpace underscores how quickly the commercial web services we use can rise and fall in popularity. With hosted life bits—one's data under one's own control—links to the materials don't rot; the data do not disappear, nor are they mined without our knowledge and consent.

As Bush imagined in 1945, everyone could have a personal piece of technology to help us remember. We would each retain the ability—and the right—to delete, to forget. "The technical aspects are somewhat challenging," Udell (2007) writes, "but the social and business aspects are even more challenging."

Personal Data Repositories

Udell, Bell, and Bush all envision personal data repositories of sorts—archives that can store information for personal recollection and research, as well as for posterity. Udell (2007) frames this as a lifetime's worth of storage, coming the closest to describing this repository as working in the service of learning. That is, he talks about how a student's repository would have to be designed to work with a school's practices and systems.

Udell is also clear that he wants to see this repository as Internet connected so that its contents can interact with all the world's knowledge, as well as with other people. That interaction, however, is always under the individual's control.

If your education-related life bits are in your own repository, you would be able to audit your education records, such as correct erroneous data and run your own analyses of data that are meaningful to you as a learner. You would have the ability to control who has access to your life bits—this is absolutely crucial. With life bits, you opt in rather than opt out of analytics and algorithms, as most technology services work now. You would be able to decide what is shared publicly, shared privately, or not shared at all. This is a deeply powerful and deeply *personal* vision of data and technology.

The World Wide Web promises us the ability to control our own domain. It promises a readable, writable web. But that's easier said than done, particularly if schools do not recognize students as having the agency to be writers and creators; instead, schools want students to be readers and consumers.

To rethink education technology demands that we rethink what we want education to do with our data. If we want to claim our domain, then we must consider who controls the space—the knowledge and the site where that is expressed online. We must work to build education technologies that place students at the center and provide them with greater control over what they do with their data and their learning.

Chapter 3
Controlling Our Own Technologies

Claiming your domain and building user-centered technologies are both attempts to get closer to what Ivan Illich calls *convivial tools*. The term comes from his 1973 book *Tools for Conviviality*, published just two years after the book he's probably best known for, *Deschooling Society* (1971). These are just two of a number of very interesting, progressive, if not radical texts about education from roughly the same period, such as Goodman's *Compulsory Mis-education and the Community of Scholars* (1964) and Postman and Weingartner's *Teaching as a Subversive Activity* (1969).

These books share the same diagnosis: our education system is controlling, exploitative, and imperialist, and despite all our talk about democratization and opportunity, school often serves to reinforce the existing hierarchies of our socioeconomic world—categorizations based on race, class, gender, and nationality.

During roughly the same period as the publication of these books challenging traditional education and traditional schooling, a growing interest emerged in what the still fairly nascent field of computing could do to hasten some of this change. Progressive education and education technology started to collide in the work of Seymour Papert

(1980) and Alan Kay (1971), for example. It's worth mentioning that in the late 1960s and early 1970s, computers were still mostly giant mainframes. And although the market for microcomputers was growing, these were largely restricted to university scientists and the military.

Kay was among those instrumental in pushing forward a vision of what we now call *personal computing*. In 1971, he published his manifesto, "A Personal Computer for Children of All Ages." Kay argues that computers will become commonplace and should be in the hands of nonprofessional users, including children. Kay describes his design for a device he calls the *Dynabook*. This device would be no larger than a notebook, weigh less than four pounds, and connect to a network—all for a price tag of five hundred dollars, which Kay insists is "not totally outrageous." (At that time, five hundred dollars was roughly the cost of a color television.) The Dynabook would be a piece of personal computing hardware that was completely programmable by its owner and by children of all ages.

"It is now within the reach of current technology to give all the Beths and their dads a 'Dynabook' to use anytime, anywhere, as they may wish," Kay (1971) writes.

> Although it can be used to communicate with others through the 'knowledge utilities' of the future such as a school 'library' (or business information system), we think that a large fraction of its use will involve reflexive communication of the owner with himself through this personal medium, much as paper and notebooks are currently used.

In Kay's vision, the ability to program a computer is powerful, not simply because computer programming is a marketable high-tech skill, but because it involves deep intellectual model building.

However, as Papert writes in his 1980 book *Mindstorms*:

> In most contemporary educational situations where children come into contact with computers, the

computer is used to put children through their paces, to provide exercises of an appropriate level of difficulty, to provide feedback, and to dispense information. The computer programming the child. (p. 19)

No doubt, that's what most education technology has become. Rather than self-directed exploration enhanced by computing devices, we find these devices used to prop up traditional school practices, ostensibly to make them more efficient. Education technology has become about control, surveillance, and data extraction. Illich, Goodman, Postman, Weingartner—none of them would be surprised to hear that, having already identified these tendencies in the very institution and practices of school itself.

But to argue that education *technology* has become about control, surveillance, and data extraction runs counter to the narrative that computer technologies are somehow better, if not liberating. We've been promised that computers will open access to information, simplify sharing, and expand our networks. In doing so, they will flatten hierarchies and connect the world.

Kay and Papert first wrote that education technologies have carried forward the talk of progressive transformation. But in practice, we see something else. Sadly, much could be said for the technology sector writ large.

Often the World Wide Web is cited as an example of what Illich (1971) calls *convivial tools*. Although his book predates the web by fifteen-plus years, Illich also speaks of *learning webs* in *Deschooling Society*. These webs, he argues, could include a rethinking of the institution of school through networks that offer the following.

1. Reference Services to Educational Objects—which facilitate access to things or processes used for formal learning
2. Skill Exchanges—which permit persons to list their skills, the conditions under which they are willing to serve as models for others who want

to learn these skills, and the addresses at which they can be reached

3. Peer-Matching—a communications network which permits persons to describe the learning activity in which they wish to engage, in the hope of finding a partner for the inquiry

4. Reference Services to Educators-at-Large—who can be listed in a directory giving the addresses and self-descriptions of professionals, paraprofessionals, and freelancers, along with conditions of access to their services (pp. 72–114)

Illich (1971) demands that we think about learning webs (networks of knowledge and learners outside of and beyond formal education institutions) and of convivial tools (technologies that can unlock these and other social services). Again, some might argue that the web does this for education. But when we put learning webs side by side with Illich's call for convivial tools, we can see how far we still need to go.

Illich's (1973) idea of convivial tools is tied to his larger critique of modern institutions. He argues that "as the power of machines increases, the role of persons more and more decreases to that of mere consumers" (p. 11). In order to build a future society that is not dominated by machines or by industry, we must:

> Learn to invert the present deep structure of tools; if we give people tools that guarantee their right to work with high, independent efficiency, thus simultaneously eliminating the need for either slaves or masters and enhancing each person's range of freedom. People need new tools to work with rather than tools that 'work' for them. They need technology to make the most of the energy and imagination each has, rather than more well-programmed energy slaves. (p. 10)

What precisely are *convivial tools*? They are easy-to-use, reliable tools, for starters. Convivial tools also should be repairable and durable. Already, we can see how the planned obsolescence of so much of technology veers away from conviviality. Convivial tools should be accessible, even free. They should be noncoercive and, according to Illich, support autonomy and agency and enhance the "graceful playfulness" in our social relationships.

In his book *Tools for Conviviality*, Illich (1973) argues that the hand tool and the telephone are convivial: "The telephone lets anybody say what he wants to the person of his choice; he can conduct business, express love, or pick a quarrel. It is impossible for bureaucrats to define what people say to each other on the phone, even though they can interfere with—or protect—the privacy of their exchange" (p. 22). Some have compared Illich's ideas about conviviality to free and open-source software. Others have claimed that convivial tools are akin to user-centered design—that is, the process of building technologies in which the needs of users are given full attention. To that, particularly when talking about tools that are convivial for learners, I would add the notion of the Indie web and claiming your domain.

The Indie Web and Edupunk

As described in the previous chapter, the Indie web movement emerged out of the growing concern about losing what was once so special and powerful about the Internet and the web—that we could build our own personal digital spaces as well as online communities. As Arizona State University journalism professor Dan Gillmor (2014) writes, "We're in danger of losing what's made the Internet the most important medium in history: a decentralized platform where the people at the edges of the networks—that would be you and me—don't need permission to communicate, create, and innovate."

The open web has increasingly become the corporate web, with powerful monopolies controlling key features like *search* and *social*, not to mention the underlying infrastructure that's always been theirs—*telecommunications*, the series of tubes themselves. We have poured our lives into Internet technologies—status updates, photos, messages, locations, fitness regimes, movie preferences, and moreover, our life bits. We have increasingly poured our lives into data silos where our personal information is now mined, value extracted from it by companies for companies.

We celebrated twenty-five years of the World Wide Web in 2014. However, web creator Tim Berners-Lee insists that it's time to redecentralize the web (Clark, 2014). That is, we should return to the web's original infrastructure and intent: not the control and centralization of information, but an opportunity for everyone to participate democratically in reading and writing online.

The Indie web movement wants just that. Centered loosely on the work of a group of developers and designers who run meet-ups and IndieWebCamps, it encourages people to become creators—not simply consumers—of web technologies and, in the process, think more carefully about what happens to their digital creations and their digital public spaces (our content and our data). It would be wrong to see this simply as nostalgia for the web we lost. It offers a different ethos from some of the web's earliest players.

The principles of the Indie web movement focus on creation and ownership. They are as follows (IndieWebCamp, 2015).

> Your content is yours. When you post something on the web, it should belong to you, not a corporation. Too many companies have gone out of business and lost all of their users' data.
>
> By joining the IndieWeb, your content stays yours and in your control.
>
> You are better connected. Your articles and status messages can go to all services, not just one, allowing you to engage with everyone. Even replies and likes on other services can come back to your site so they're all in one place.
>
> You are in control. You can post anything you want, in any format you want, with no one monitoring you.

> In addition, you share simple readable links such as example.com/ideas.
>
> These links are permanent and will always work.

The Indie web posits itself as an alternative to the philosophy, the funding, and even the technologies of the corporate web, but it could provide a powerful alternative to much of education technology as well, which is committed to controlling and monetizing students' and teachers' connections, content, and data.

The Indie web isn't the only point of resistance to that control, of course. It is kin to *Edupunk* perhaps, a word first used by UMW's Jim Groom in 2008 to describe "the necessity for a communal vision of EdTech to fight capital's will to power at the expense of community." Often positioned as an argument against the LMS and other institutionally mandated education technologies that lock students' work and data into online silos, Edupunk carries with it a do-it-yourself (DIY) ethos. It's an ethos deeply connected to claiming your domain.

In a 2014 article in *EDUCAUSE Review Online*, "Reclaiming Innovation," Jim Groom and Brian Lamb suggest:

> Rather than continuing to yell about the state of MOOCs and LMSs, perhaps it's more useful to turn to Jon Udell's ideas first expressed seven years ago. In his talk "The Disruptive Nature of Technology," Udell laid out a vision in which K–12, colleges/universities, and open-source programmers are encouraged to help learners create "coherent personal digital archives" that seamlessly integrate with a wide range of institutional systems.
>
> Udell argued that these archives should encompass more than just a student's schoolwork; they should also include personal photos, videos, transcripts, X-rays, dental records, police records, and a million other digital life-bits. The archives should then grow into much larger, abstracted digital spaces in which people manage and maintain all their records and

also decide how to push out their records appropriately to various destinations.

Although we're currently nowhere near this idea, how can businesses, educational institutions, and governments alike not consider the importance of giving individuals control over their digital archives? Or their learning analytics data? Open formats such as XML and RSS have opened the door, but they're just a first step to a solution that will require our insistence on and commitment to imagining coherent, aggregated hubs of content and functionality that we each can own and manage.

Or, as some in the Indie web put it, "Publish on your own site, syndicate everywhere" (POSSE) (IndieWebCamp, 2015).

A Domain of One's Own

But first, of course, you must own your own site. I repeat this often: one of the most important initiatives in education technology is UMW's Domain of One's Own. This program was first piloted by the university's Division of Teaching and Learning Technologies, where Groom is executive director. Other universities have since launched similar programs, including Emory University, the University of Oklahoma, and Davidson College.

As mentioned, the Domain of One's Own gives students and staff their own web domains—not simply a bit of web space at the university's .edu, but their own domains. UMW facilitates the purchase of each domain, helps with installation of WordPress (and other open-source software), offers support—technical *and* instructional—and hosts the site until graduation. And then, contrary to what happens with an LMS, for example, students are able take the domains and their contents with them. It is, after all, *their* education, *their* content, *their* data—*their own domain.*

The Domain of One's Own initiative at UMW purposefully invokes Virginia Woolf's (1929) *A Room of One's Own*: "A woman must have money, and a room of her own, if she is to write fiction" (p. 6). That is, one needs a space—a safe space that one controls—in order to be intellectually productive.

Intellectual productivity on the web looks a bit different, no doubt, than it did at Woolf's writing desk. But there remains this idea, deeply embedded in the Domain of One's Own project, that it is important to have one's own space in order to develop one's ideas and one's craft. It's important that, as learners, we have control over our content and our data. We aren't simply receptacles for content delivery mechanisms, as imaged by the machines of programmed instruction. And we aren't simply the sources for learning outcomes and learning analytics—data that can be used to feed the new algorithms of today's fancier teaching machines.

Having one's own domain means too that we have much more say over what we present to the world in terms of our public profiles, professional portfolios, and digital identities. It means control over the look and feel of our own sites and control over the content. It means control over what's shared and a bit more control over one's personal data.

Domains and the Democratization of Knowledge

Own your own domain, Edupunk tells us. But that's easier said than done.

Despite all the talk about the democratization of knowledge and publishing, thanks to technologies like the World Wide Web, most of us still don't have the skills—or don't believe we have the skills—to manage our own technical infrastructure on or offline.

There's much talk of new technologies demanding new literacies. These new literacies might include activities like text messaging, blogging, social networking, podcasting, video making—creating and saying things with computers. These new literacies include computer programming too, such as understanding how the ones and zeroes work, how the hardware works, how the software works, and how the networking works.

No doubt, many computer technologies are poised to alter and extend our communication abilities, blending text, sound, imagery, and data in new ways. Although connected to older analog practices, these technologies quite arguably do change what it means to both read and write texts—that is, they change our concept of what it means to be literate. (And they change the meaning of *text* as well.)

The rise of any new literacies needed to wield these new technologies effectively places demands on all of us. And while there is concern that schools aren't doing enough to teach programming, for example, failure to attain these new literacies does not only affect students. We are *all* expected to move much more quickly to identify problems; know where to find information to help us address those problems, often on our own; evaluate and synthesize information from a number of sources to try to solve those problems; communicate with others about problems and potential solutions; monitor the solutions we've found; and stay up-to-date with new issues as they arise.

We are increasingly expected to accomplish these tasks via the Internet and to address elements of our professional and personal lives online. We do this as students, teachers, workers, and citizens alike. But again—the refrain of this book—how many of these tasks and their outcomes do we control?

Understanding how these new technologies work should include the ability to manage one's own website—one's own domain. The web has been around since 1989. It seems that knowing how to build a web page using hypertext markup language (HTML), the language of the web, would be more commonplace by now. But arguably, since the web's early years, building web pages and participating in the construction of websites has actually become more difficult. Blogging software has become more powerful, but in many ways it's also become more complicated and more complex.

Having one's own website, once one of the promises offered by the World Wide Web, has moved beyond most people's reach. Building a website has become more and more professionalized, and the necessary skills for doing so aren't particularly accessible to the general public. Running your own site has long meant running your own server, understanding web hosting and domain name servers (DNS), having access to file transfer protocol (FTP), understanding and having access to a database such as MySQL, and so on. This can all sound incredibly intimidating to someone who's unsure of his or her of technological know-how, and it never helps that software engineers say things like, "This is easy," when the step-by-step instructions read as gobbledygook.

Just as Berners-Lee calls for us to "redecentralize the web" (Clark, 2014), we also should think about how we can "redecomplexify" it. Again, to use Illich's conceptualization of tools, this would bring the web much closer to conviviality—easy to use, openly accessible, durable, and reliable, and working in the service of autonomy and agency.

Owning your own domain does not have to be complicated, nor should a demand for easy-to-use technologies stop us from having more control and understanding of the tools we use. Apple is known for the phrase *It just works*, but computers don't *just work*.

We also need to recognize that, as Illich (1973) emphasizes, convivial tools and a convivial society must go hand-in-hand. There is no technological fix to make education better. It's a political problem, not just a technological one. We cannot develop technologies that address systemic inequalities, created by and reinscribed by education, unless we are willing to confront those inequalities head on.

Those radical education writers of the 1960s and 1970s offered powerful diagnoses about what was wrong with schools. Progressive education technologists of the same period imagined ways in which ed-tech could possibly dismantle some of the school drudgery and exploitation at which those writers pointed their fingers.

But decades later, where are we now? Instead of liberation, we have LinkedIn. We find ourselves with technologies working to make that exploitation and centralization of power even more entrenched. There must be alternatives—both within and without technology and within and without institutions. Those of us who talk, write, and teach education technology must pursue those technologies that serve learners' needs, not promote consumption and further institutional and industrial control. In Illich's (1973) words, "The crisis I have described confronts people with a choice between convivial tools and being crushed by machines" (p. 4).

We must do better so that students—and all of us—have the capacity to program not (as Papert suggested) to be programmed by these powerful machines.

Conclusion

What happens when you google yourself? When you search for your name online, what is the first link that shows up? The second? The third? What's on the first page of results? What photos appear? What information is the most readily available about you online? And what does this say about you? Are you happy with it? What do you do if you're not? What happens when an employer googles a student who is applying for a job or applying for college?

The answers to these questions, particularly in schools, are often framed in terms of *digital citizenship*—what one needs to know in order to use technology appropriately. We caution one another about what we post online, for example, to Facebook, Instagram, and Twitter. The tenor of this conversation is often tinged with fears that people will see students doing or saying "bad things." Rarely do we give students the opportunity to demonstrate the good work that they do publicly. And even more rarely do schools give students the opportunity to decide how that looks. Rarely do digital citizenship conversations probe the appropriateness of the demands on our data and content that technology companies increasingly make.

Outside of school, many students have developed rich social lives online where they develop their digital identities. I use the plural *identities* here, because we all have multiple identities that we wield on- and offline. That is, we might act one way on Facebook because we know our grandmother is there. We might act one way in an LMS because we recognize that our participation is being assessed. We might act another way when we post videos to YouTube and yet another if we're sending private video messages through an app like Snapchat. All of these posts leave data trails strewn across the Internet. The challenge for us all is to gain control over our actions, words, images, and data online.

The vast amount of data mining that's taking place, the claims to our intellectual property, and the lack of control over our digital materials are all good reasons for claiming our domain. Young people interact with different identities online just as they're in the very serious process of developing their real identities—these are reasons to make sure that they get to do this in ways that are not exploited, mined, or shared without their control.

At the simplest level—or at least the reason that's least likely to give people pause—providing learners with the opportunity to control their domain helps them build their own digital portfolios. Digital portfolios can be used in a classroom setting for students to demonstrate their learning. These portfolios can contain text, images, and video and audio recordings, giving students opportunities to express themselves in a variety of ways beyond the traditional pen-and-paper test or essay.

When students control their portfolios—what they contain and what they look like—they have a great deal more ownership over how they display their work and their identities online. Inevitably, a certain vulnerability comes with learning in public and displaying this information online. But giving students control over those data is important and empowering.

A digital portfolio can be like that manila envelope my mother saved for me. It can be a way to track growth and demonstrate new learning over the course of a student's school career. However, a digital portfolio must be in a format that remains available and accessible to the student—it doesn't necessarily make it into a student's own digital manila envelope. In other words, the digital portfolio's content shouldn't be locked away in a proprietary system controlled by the school. As a student moves from grade to grade and from school to school, the portfolio *must* be able to travel with him or her.

Education technology—and more broadly, education practices—does a terrible job with this sort of portability and interoperability. When a student moves to a new school, for example, he or she often has to request his or her transcript, a document that lists the student's courses and grades. A transcript is by definition a copy of his or her education record. The transcript is often printed on a piece of paper with formal letterhead, perhaps with a watermark or stamp to show that it's official. A transcript is only portable insofar as the student carries it or mails it (or keeps it in a manila envelope).

This lack of portability continues with most digital schoolwork as well. Even if students are encouraged to create online portfolios or to use services like Google Apps for Education to store all their work, they don't actually get to take that work with them when they move or graduate. (In the case of Google Apps, you can download your files, but then you need to find a new place to store them.) Too often, students' work in these systems gets deleted over the summer months, as schools aren't in the business of permanently storing student work. School district IT is not the right steward for student work; it should be the students and their parents or guardians.

Creating a digital portfolio is, therefore, really just a first step in this broader claiming project. It's an important step, but we still need to work harder to give students the most effective tools to *own their own digital domain*—not just the work that would be displayed in a final project portfolio. They must own all of it—all their data, all their metadata, and all their content—the data that software treats as mineable, and the data that schools think are meaningless.

Beyond the Portfolio

Lots of books are available containing practical advice for how educators can integrate digital portfolios into their classrooms. This isn't meant to be one of those books. Admittedly, it's not much of a practical book at all. A lot of the ideas I've explored here are, as Udell and others have noted, perhaps technologically feasible but require major shifts in the business and politics of the technology industry. The Facebooks and Googles of the world aren't particularly interested in you owning your own domain. They want you to share and store your content and data with them. Their business model—advertising and data mining—demands it. To claim your domain in an educational setting also requires a major shift in schooling and in the practices associated with both education technology and education as a whole.

Instead, this book attempts to outline how me might start to think about alternative education technologies—those that aren't reliant on data mining, for example. But that doesn't mean that there aren't some practical steps that everyone can take right now in order to get closer to claiming their domain.

Following are a few of those steps.

- Conduct an inventory of all your data. Where do you store your photos? Where do you store your notes? Conduct an inventory of all the applications that you use. Close any accounts you do not use.

- Publish on your own site and syndicate everywhere. Claiming your domain doesn't mean that you need to shut down your Facebook account or refuse to share photos on Instagram. But make sure you have a record of what you've done, what you've said, and what you've built.

- Keep a copy of all your original files. You can store them on an external hard drive or in the cloud.

- Use technologies that offer interoperability. Make sure that once you enter your data or content, you also can

- *remove* your data or content. (And make sure that they come out in a format that's actually usable by other applications.)
- Review the terms of service for the applications you use. Do not use services that have onerous terms (such as those that make sweeping claims to your intellectual property or that have few protections for your data). Review the privacy policies for the applications you use. What happens to your data? With whom are they shared? How long are they stored?

And finally . . .

- *Buy your own domain.* Buy domains for your children. Remember, having your own domain does not mean that you must have a blog. You can create a single-page app or a single-page website. (Find out more about this and other resources in the appendix, page 51.)

Claim Is a Verb

My mom gave me a manila envelope containing a selection of my schoolwork. I have another file folder that contains my college transcripts. Together, these folders contain all the official records of my formal education. Together, both contain just a fraction of the work I've accomplished as a learner.

Now that we use more and more technologies in order to teach and learn, it's possible that we can retain a better picture of what we've done, studied, created, and written. It's possible, but it's not happening. Instead, neither parents nor students are likely to be able to pull together a manila envelope showcasing what a student learns. Education data are trapped in software silos. They're not accessible to students, although they're increasingly mined by the software companies themselves.

How do we reclaim education technology so that it is not simply a new frontier for these sorts of data extraction efforts? How do we reclaim education technology so it can provide a place for students to control their data, their content, their learning, and their identities—and develop them without being probed or profiled?

At this point, I'm not sure we can. But I think we must quickly figure out ways to make this happen. We cannot surrender to the newest narratives that more data collection and data mining will promote what's best for students. All of us must have more input into what happens to our data. All of us must be able to decide what we want to preserve and protect, share, and delete. They're our data. They're our learning.

As we think about what it means to move education from the analog to the digital, we must seize the opportunity to rethink much about the practices of education, education technology, and technology as a whole.

How do we rewire all these systems so that they are less exploitative and more progressive? The first step—for all of us—is to determine how best to claim our own domains, including our knowledge, expertise, identities, places, and spaces in, on, and with technology.

Appendix

The challenge of any book about technology is that technologies are constantly changing and evolving, whereas books fix information in print. I'm reluctant to make too detailed a list of products and services that you can use to claim your domain for fear of immediately dating this book. Once it's published, there will no doubt be additional or alternative apps available. But then again, I don't want a list of resources to be so vague that it is useless.

This appendix includes definitions of some of the more important terms one needs to know in order to claim his or her domain. It's followed by a list of recommended resources.

Definitions

Domain: A domain name is used to identify a "place" on the Internet.

Domain name system (DNS): This system translates human-readable web addresses into IP addresses.

Transmission control protocol/Internet protocol (TCP/IP): This is the basic communication language or protocol of the Internet.

File transfer protocol (FTP): FTP is used to move computer files from one host to another over TCP.

Host: A host is the name for a computer connected to the Internet. Hosting services provide space on a server that others can lease. These servers can both manage file storage and serve up web content.

Hypertext markup language (HTML): HTML is the standard markup language used to create web pages.

Cascading style sheets (CSS): This style sheet language is used for describing the look and formatting of a document written for the web.

Single-page application: A single-page application (app) is a web application or website that fits on a single web page. Typically, a single-page app is comprised of HTML, CSS, and JavaScript.

Syndication: Web syndication is a form of syndication in which website material is made available to multiple other sites. Most commonly, this refers to the process of making web feeds (updates to a website or blog) available through a subscription. This is known as rich site summary (RSS).

Interoperability: This is the ability of making systems and organizations work together. When applied to technology, it is the ability of systems to share formats, languages, and data models.

Intellectual property: This legal term refers to creative works and acts, including music, literature, and invention. While laws are in place that ostensibly protects creators and their work—copyright and patents, for example—it is important to remember that these have their origins in a predigital world. Many aspects of intellectual property are challenged by the move to digital because it makes the process of copying so very easy.

Resources

A Domain of One's Own: The domain and web space offered by the University of Mary Washington (UMW) to each staff member and student, "encouraging individuals to explore the creation and development of their digital identities" (A Domain of One's Own, n.d.). You can find more information about A Domain of One's Own at http://umw.domains/.

Blog: A blog, short for *weblog*, is a presentation of articles on a site in reverse chronological order. Blogs emerged in the late 1990s alongside the web, and they are intertwined with the notion that the web enables a democratization of publishing. Since then, a number of blogging platforms have been released, but not all of them allow people to own and write in their own domains. WordPress is a free and open-source blogging tool and a content management system based on PHP and MySQL. It is, arguably, one of the most popular blogging platforms. Users can either use WordPress sites for blogging or the software from Wordpress.org to run a blog on their own site.

Storage: A file hosting service, cloud storage service, online file storage provider, or cyberlocker is an Internet hosting service specifically designed to host and store user files. It allows users to upload files that could then be accessed over the Internet from a different computer, tablet, smartphone, or other networked device by the same user, or possibly other users, after providing a password or other authentication.

Indie web: The Indie web, detailed in chapter 3, has a website at http://indiewebcamp.com/ where you can read about its principles, which include the key maxim: *Your content is yours*. For use in education, the Indie web might include a personal data locker, as prototyped by the Locker Project (http://lockerproject.org/), where you can safely store your data and share it on your own terms. It also might include a service like Known (https://withknown.com/), which offers open-source technology for publishing and syndicating social media materials, including photos and status updates, to other sites in addition to your own.

Terms of Service; Didn't Read (ToS;DR): This website is a crowd-sourced attempt to translate web companies' terms of service into a readable, understandable, and rateable format. You may access the website at https://tosdr.org/.

Web hosting: A web hosting service is a type of Internet hosting service that allows individuals and organizations to make their websites accessible via the World Wide Web. Web hosts are companies that provide space on a server owned or leased for use by clients, as well as providing Internet connectivity, typically in a data center. Web hosts can also provide data center space and connectivity to the Internet for other servers located in their data center.

References and Resources

Anderson, C., & Wolff, M. (2010, August 17). The web is dead. Long live the Internet. *Wired*. Accessed at www.wired.com /2010/08/ff_webrip/all on March 15, 2015.

Bush, V. (1945, July 1). As we may think. *The Atlantic Monthly*. Accessed at www.theatlantic.com/magazine/archive/1945/07/as -we-may-think/303881 on March 13, 2015.

Case, A. (2011). Templated self. In *A dictionary of cyborg anthropology*. Accessed at http://cyborganthropology.com/Templated_Self on March 13, 2015.

Clark, L. (2014, February 6). Tim Berners-Lee: We need to re-decentralise the web. *Wired* 6. Accessed at www.wired.co .uk/news/archive/2014–02/06/tim-berners-lee-reclaim-the-web on March 15, 2015.

Dash, A. (2012a, December 18). *Rebuilding the web we lost*. Accessed at http://dashes.com/anil/2012/12/rebuilding-the-web-we-lost .html on March 13, 2015.

Dash, A. (2012b, December 13). *The web we lost*. Accessed at http:// dashes.com/anil/2012/12/the-web-we-lost.html on March 15, 2012.

A Domain of One's Own. (2015). Accessed at http://umw.domains/ on July 31, 2015.

Freire, P. (1970). *Pedagogy of the oppressed* [M. B. Ramos, trans]. New York: Continuum.

Gillmor, D. (2014, April 25). *Why the Indie web movement is so important*. Accessed at http://dangillmor.com/2014/04/25/indie -web-important on March 13, 2015.

Goodman, P. (1964). *Compulsory mis-education and the community of scholars*. New York: Horizon Press.

Groom, J. (2008, May 25). The glass bees. *Bava Tuesdays*. Accessed at http://bavatuesdays.com/the-glass-bees on March 13, 2015.

Groom, J., & Lamb, B. (2014). Reclaiming innovation. *EDUCAUSE Review Online*. Accessed at www.educause.edu/visuals/shared/er/extras/2014/ReclaimingInnovation/default.html on March 13, 2015.

Holt, J. (1969). *The underachieving school*. New York: Pitman Publishing.

IBM. (n.d.). *What is big data?* Accessed at www-01.ibm.com/software/data/bigdata/what-is-ibig-data.html on March 13, 2015.

Illich, I. (1971). *Deschooling society*. London: Marion Boyars.

Illich, I. (1973). *Tools for conviviality*. London: Marion Boyars.

IndieWebCamp. (2015). *What is the IndieWeb?* Accessed at https://indiewebcamp.com on March 15, 2015.

Kay, A. (1971). *A personal computer for children of all ages*. Accessed at www.mprove.de/diplom/gui/kay72.html on March 13, 2015.

Known. (2015). Accessed at https://withknown.com on July 6, 2015.

Kozol, J. (1967). *Death at an early age: The destruction of the hearts and minds of Negro children in the Boston public schools*. Boston: Houghton Mifflin.

Kranzberg, M. (1986). Technology and history: "Kranzberg's laws." *Technology and Culture, 27*(3), 544–560.

The Locker Project. (n.d.). Accessed at http://lockerproject.org on July 6, 2015.

May, K. T. (2012, July 18). *Completely free online classes? Coursera.org now offering courses from 16 top colleges*. Accessed at http://blog.ted.com/completely-free-online-classes-coursera-org-now-offering-courses-from-14-top-colleges on March 13, 2015.

Microsoft Research. (2015). *MyLifeBits*. Accessed at http://research.microsoft.com/en-us/projects/mylifebits on March 13, 2015.

Owens, T. (2014). *Designing online communities: How designers, developers, community managers, and software structure discourse and knowledge production on the web*. New York: Peter Lang.

Palmer, M. (2006, November 3). *Data is the new oil.* Accessed at http://ana.blogs.com/maestros/2006/11/data_is_the_new.html on March 13, 2015.

Papert, S. (1980). *Mindstorms: Children, computers, and powerful ideas.* New York: Basic Books.

Postman, N., & Weingartner, C. (1969). *Teaching as a subversive activity.* New York: Delacorte Press.

Reimer, E. W. (1971). *School is dead: An essay on alternatives in education.* London: Penguin.

Solon, O. (2011, September 21). You are Facebook's product, not customer. *Wired UK.* Accessed at www.wired.co.uk/news/archive/2011–09/21/doug-rushkoff-hello-etsy on March 13, 2015.

Terms of Service, Didn't Read. (n.d.) Accessed at https://tosdr.org on July 6, 2015.

Thorp, J. (2012). Big data is not the new oil. *Harvard Business Review.* Accessed at https://hbr.org/2012/11/data-humans-and-the-new-oil on March 13, 2015.

Tucker, P. (2013, May 7). Has big data made anonymity impossible? *MIT Technology Review.* Accessed at www.technologyreview.com/news/514351/has-big-data-made-anonymity-impossible on March 15, 2015.

Udell, J. (2007, May 22). *Hosted lifebits.* Accessed at http://blog.jonudell.net/2007/05/22/hosted-lifebits on March 13, 2015.

United States Department of Education. (n.d.). *FERPA general guidance for students.* Accessed at www2.ed.gov/policy/gen/guid/fpco/ferpa/students.html on July 23, 2015.

Woolf, V. (1929). *A room of one's own.* Eastford, CT: Martino Fine Books.

World Education University. (n.d.). *Web privacy policy.* Accessed at www.theweu.com/privacy on March 13, 2015.

Solutions for Modern Learning

Solutions Series: Solutions for Modern Learning engages K–12 educators in a powerful conversation about learning and schooling in the connected world. In a short, reader-friendly format, these books challenge traditional thinking about education and help to develop the modern contexts teachers and leaders need to effectively support digital learners.

Claim Your Domain—And Own Your Online Presence
Audrey Watters
BKF687

The End of School as We Know It
Bruce Dixon
BKF692

Freedom to Learn
Will Richardson
BKF688

Gearing Up for Learning Beyond K–12
Bryan Alexander
BKF693

Make School Meaningful—And Fun!
Roger C. Schank
BKF686

The New Pillars of Modern Teaching
Gayle Allen
BKF685

Wait! Your professional development journey doesn't have to end with the last pages of this book.

We realize improving student learning doesn't happen overnight. And your school or district shouldn't be left to puzzle out all the details of this process alone.

No matter where you are on the journey, we're committed to helping you get to the next stage.

Take advantage of everything from **custom workshops** to **keynote presentations** and **interactive web and video conferencing**. We can even help you develop an action plan tailored to fit your specific needs.

Let's get the conversation started.

Call 888.763.9045 today.

solution-tree.com